VIPER

Matt Stone

Motorbooks International
Publishers & Wholesalers ®

Dedication

To the memory of the late Dean Batchelor, one of my mentors in the journalism biz;
to my friends of the Motor Press Guild; and to the members of Team Viper, who put this snake on the road.

First published in 1996 by Motorbooks International
Publishers & Wholesalers, 729 Prospect Avenue,
PO Box 1, Osceola, WI 54020-0001 USA

Motorbooks International books are also available at
discounts in bulk quantity for industrial or sales-
promotional use. For details write to Special Sales
Manager at the Publisher's address

Library of Congress Cataloging-in-Publication Data

Stone, Matt L.
    Viper / Matt L. Stone.
      p. cm. – (Enthusiasts color series)
    Includes bibliographical references and index.
    ISBN 0-7603-0149-2 (pbk.)
    1. Viper automobile. I. Title II. Series.
TL215.V544S76   1996
629.222'2--dc20   96-14074

On the front cover: David Newhardt photographed this
1996 Viper RT/10 prototype at Southern California's
Willow Springs Raceway.

On the frontispiece: Viper GTS Coupe and RT/10
roadster by Gene Garfinkle, IDSA. This new and
previously unpublished work was rendered in pastels and
markers on vellum paper. Garfinkle, an Art Center
College graduate and former GM Design staffer, has
been involved in automotive design and illustration for
more than 40 years.

On the title page: The genesis of American high-performance. This John Lamm photo, taken in 1992 at the former Hill & Vaughn restoration facility in Southern
California, shows a 1992 Viper surrounded by a Ford
GT40, Shelby 427 Cobra, *Ol' Yaller* special, Kurtis 500,
and Scarab.

On the back cover: Production-spec 1996 GTS Coupe shot
at the Chrysler proving grounds in Arizona. *Bill Delaney*

Printed in Hong Kong

Contents

Acknowledgments

My sincere thanks first and foremost to the Viper's "Fourfathers": Bob Lutz, Chrysler president and chief operating officer; Tom Gale, Chrysler vice president of product design and international operations; Francois Castaing, vice president of vehicle engineering and general manager of powertrain operations; and the legendary Carroll Shelby, performance consultant to the Viper Project. A special appreciation to Mr. Lutz and Mr. Shelby, who set time aside from their furious schedules to chat with me about the Viper—as did Roy Sjoberg, executive engineer of the Viper Project; Ron Smith, vice president of Dodge marketing; and Pete Gladysz, Team Viper chassis manager.

Author Matt Stone

Assembling the background information and archival artwork, and arranging the shooting of new photography and access to Viper cars for this project were all made possible by many current and former members of Chrysler's Product Public Relations staff, including Tom Kowaleski, director of product PR, and especially Terri Houtman, manager of corporate image and brand PR. Others included Lindsay Brooke, Michael Coates, Pamela Mahoney, Stephanie Harris, Jeff Leestma, Kari St. Antoine, Art Ponter of the Chrysler Archives, and others who no doubt contributed behind the scenes. The copyrighted materials and trademarks contained herein are reprinted and used with permission from Chrysler Corporation, which owns the copyright for same.

Several of the profession's best photographers fixed their lenses on Vipers for this project: the incomparable John Lamm; racer/designer/legend/friend Peter Brock; David W. Newhardt, with whom this is my second project; fellow *AutoWeek* contributor Bill Delaney; and Scott Mead, a promising newcomer. Our thanks as well to those folks whose cars were "snapped" along the way, but whose names are unknown to us.

Other folks and firms who helped in one way or another: Rick Roso, PR manager for Skip Barber Driving School; John Hennessey of Hennessey Motorsports; John Thompson of J. R. Thompson Company; Lee Corsack of Visual Graphics of New England; fellow journalist Chris Poole for proofreading and fact checking; Mike, Jean, Jeff, and the gang at Flaggs Photo Center; and Tom Lindamood and his crew at A & M Specialists West. A special tip of the hat to friend and artist Gene Garfinkle who created the frontispiece artwork.

Thanks again to my editor, Zack Miller, and all the professionals at Motorbooks International.

Deepest appreciation to my wife, Linda, and all the rest of my family and friends for putting up with all this car nonsense that continues to be one of my great passions in life.

—*Matt Stone*

INTRODUCTION

The mere fact that the Viper exists today as a production vehicle is nothing short of amazing. Building cars is tough business these days: Society demands they be recyclable, biodegradable, nonpolluting, economical, safe-as-armor, and politically correct (whatever that means). Auto makers need to satisfy a million government regulations and agencies, their own accountants and stockholders, and (somehow) the people who buy their product. This environment has helped create many supremely competent but hopelessly boring cars. Yet in the midst of this sea of seemingly red-tape-bound mediocrity, Dodge issues forth a 488-cubic-inch, two-seat roadster that will break most speed limits in any of its six gears. As of this writing, it has no door handles, roll-up windows, or airbags. Credit Chrysler Corporation's vision and guts in producing a vehicle designed and single-mindedly focused on performance, individuality, and driving pleasure—at a price tag not even approaching six figures.

The Viper also served as the pilot within Chrysler for the cross-functional "team" approach to developing and producing cars, a philosophy that has proliferated throughout the company (and other auto makers) as a better way to get the job done. The significance of Team Viper cannot be overemphasized as a *major* element in the car's aura and success.

I am not at this time a Viper owner, but I have put in many a mile at the wheel, and I have enjoyed them immensely. I also enjoy the infectious enthusiasm shared by Viper owners. Don't bother them with talk of the 1960s or any other era: For them, *these* are the Good Old Days.

This is certainly not an all-encompassing volume on the Viper, as our space here is limited; future books will be written, and the story continues. It is my intention to author a more in-depth work on the Viper by the end of the decade. For now though, I hope you enjoy this look at the Viper's beginnings, its first five years as a production car, the ripple effect it has had on other Chrysler products, and what the next generation—evolving just as we go to press—has in store. Thank you for purchasing *Viper!*

CHAPTER ONE

VIPER GENESIS

"I sat down with Lutz and we
talked about how we oughta
build a sport car. . . ."
—*Carroll Shelby*

Chrysler might have been the last American company you would expect to set out and build an elemental, high-performance roadster such as the Viper. Both Ford and General Motors have had extensive history with sporting performance. Ford has won LeMans and has powered Indy 500 winners; Chevrolet has built what was (at the time) rightly called "America's Only True Sports Car," the Corvette. But the smolderings at Chrysler were there, and were probably first recognizable after World War II. At

This styling concept drawing shows that the makings of the overall shape, rear sport bar, and hood-mounted exhaust vents were already in place in late 1988. *Team Viper*

No top, no side windows, no door handles, but Chrysler powered and made in the USA: The Cunningham formula certainly provided inspiration for the Viper-to-be. Bumpers appear to be an afterthought, and numbers indicate that this Cunningham saw its fair share of SCCA racing in the early 1950s. This photograph was taken in August 1951, about 40 years prior to the first production Viper RT/10s. *Chrysler*

A Chrysler Hemi as installed in the '51 Cunningham roadster. The four single-choke carburetors are Zenith units. *Chrysler*

least two factors set the stage for its postwar performance awakening: the Hemi V-8 and chief stylist Virgil Exner.

The Fire Power Hemi V-8, first introduced in 1951, gave Chrysler a modern, overhead-valve V-8 with exceptional performance potential; indeed its basic architecture is still found in today's supercharged, nitro-burning NHRA Top Fuel and Funny Car drag racers, with outputs exceeding 3,000 horsepower. It was called

10

THE ORIGINAL SNAKE: CARROLL SHELBY

Carroll Shelby poses with a Viper prototype at Indianapolis Motor Speedway. Shelby provided a good deal of input on what the Viper should and shouldn't be. This is not the car that would ultimately pace the 1991 race. Note that the headlight covers do not cut into the top part of bumper and that no Viper badge is on the nose. *Chrysler*

As one of the "Fourfathers," Carroll Shelby played an integral and inspirational role in the Viper's development. The ancestral connection to the Shelby 427 Cobra comes through loud and clear. I spoke with Carroll in July 1995 to gain some insight on how this legendary race driver and car constructor feels about his relationship with Chrysler, and about the Viper itself. Here are some excerpts:

Author: You were awaiting a heart transplant during the planning and development stages of the Viper. Please describe your involvement with the car.

Shelby: I went to all the Viper meetings for about the first year and a half, and then it got so that I couldn't go anymore, waiting for a heart. All I ever did was keep preaching, "Let's keep the weight down; keep the weight down,"

'cause when you start building something like that inside of a big corporation, weight is always a problem . . . my main input into the thing is that I sat down with Lutz and he said, "Let's build us a sport-car." He wanted to put the V-10 in it; I wanted to put the V-8 in it, and he won. The main contribution I made, besides the Cobra, you know, it being a modern Cobra, was working with Iacocca and meeting with him about every two weeks . . . we were moving into a recession, and to keep him OK and writing checks every two weeks [for the Viper program]. . . .

Author: Considering the environment in large automotive corporations, I think it's impressive the Viper ever got built.

Shelby: When people ask me about the Viper, when they say, "Oh, it has no roll-up windows," or when they're critical of the Viper, I say, "If you knew what we had to go through, what Bob Lutz and I had to go through with Iacocca, just to get him to let us build it, then you realize how badly we needed to change the image of Chrysler, you'd never say a critical word about it." . . .

Author: What about the Viper would you change?

Shelby: Oh, I'd whack 500 pounds off of it, but I'm not going to say that in a critical sort of way because I don't think that if the corporation sat down and started to build the car again, with all the givens that they have and all they have to put in the car, I don't think they could save over 300 pounds. . . .

Author: The Cobra had an approximate six-model-year production life. How long would you envision the Viper to be a viable, marketable piece?

Shelby: It's just according to how greedy they get! If they would build 250 cars a year, it would last for 15 years, but they aren't going to do that. They're going to saturate the market; the bean counters will take the place of common sense every time.

The second-generation 426 Hemi V-8 ruled the roads and the drag strips of the 1960s. Just one example of the many Chrysler muscle cars to carry "The Elephant" motor was this '67 Dodge Charger. *Chrysler*

This early rendering testifies that many of Viper's styling elements were cast early on, such as glinting headlight cover shape, bulging rear fenders and low-cut windshield. *Team Viper*

"Hemi," owing to its hemispheric combustion chambers, which placed the spark plug in the center of the combustion chamber for more efficient burning and better performance. The engine grew to 392 cubic inches by the end of the 1950s.

Exner, a talented and flamboyant stylist, had come to Chrysler from Studebaker in 1950. He admired the design talent and coachbuilding ability of the Italian styling houses, or *carrozzeria*, particularly that of Ghia. Ghia designed and constructed a number of styling exercises, or "Idea Cars" as they were often referred to at the time, for Chrysler, all of which possessed decidedly sporting flavor: the Plymouth Explorer, the Chrysler K-310 and C-200, the Chrysler Falcon, and a series of machines dubbed Firearrow. Several of these machines featured Hemi V-8 power. Though none made production per se, they had some

The Viper show car on display at the Detroit auto show in 1989. Crowd—and media—reaction was overwhelming, confirming what Chrysler was no doubt hoping to hear: The demand and the market was there. *Team Viper*

influence on Chrysler design throughout the 1950s and into the early 1960s.

The Hemi's first real foray into a "production" sports car was not in a Chrysler product at all, but a very American effort nonetheless at the hands of race driver, team owner, yachtsman, and car constructor Briggs Swift Cunningham. Cunningham had done reasonably well at the 1950 24 Hours of LeMans endurance race in France with two Cadillac-powered

entries; he once commented that "the French welcomed us to come back, but said to bring smaller cars." He began building his own Cunningham racers and limited-production street cars in Palm Beach, Florida, and turned to Chrysler's Hemi for power. Cunningham's racing creations were mostly taut roadsters, bodied by Italy's Vignale; they were truly the American Ferraris of their day. In the case of the C4-R, for example, the Hemi was tuned to deliver

ROY H. SJOBERG, EXECUTIVE ENGINEER, ON TEAM VIPER

The Wisdom of teams: Team Viper poses with the VM-01 prototype. *Team Viper*

"It's really the basic foundation: teamwork. The Viper was truly Chrysler's pilot for the cross-functional team. I believe the key to the Viper product is the Viper Team, not any one individual, other than our sponsor, Bob Lutz. It's been the team functioning together, coming to understand each other. Not always agreeing, and it's not always been happy times; there have been frustrating times. The evolution of that has brought what I believe is an excellent sports car, an American sports car.

"There are five keys to good teamwork that Viper has.

"Number one is vision, and Bob Lutz gave us the vision. Bob Lutz, Tom Gale, and Francois Castaing gave us that vision. Number two is product passion . . . everyone on the team has that product passion, and it can overcome a lot of roadblocks. Third is that it's a Team that's *hands-on*. Nobody steers the car from behind the desk. We are all hands-on, working on the product, understanding the product, from the craftsperson to the executive of the project, which is me. Fourth, which has been really key . . . is the empowerment, and the acceptance of risk. In a large company, bureaucracy can overrun a small skunk works like we are. Management that empowers and accepts risk is paramount to success. Last is management by coaching. Those are the five keys to 'How did Chrysler do it?' and why the car is what it is."

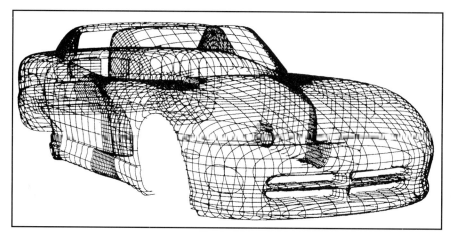

A CAD/CAM rendering of an early Viper RT/10 body shell. *Chrysler*

more than 300 horsepower, and C4-Rs were often clocked at well over 150 miles per hour.

Cunningham also produced handsome coupes and roadsters for the street, in an effort to help support the racing venture. The first C-2s were constructed in 1952, and the final C-6 models in 1955, with most being Chrysler powered. Though Briggs Cunningham never did achieve his goal of building and driving the first American car to win LeMans, he had racing successes at other venues. Cunningham would continue to compete successfully in Jaguars, OSCAs, Maseratis, and Corvettes. Still, when searching for the Viper's earliest roots, you need only look as far as, say, a Cunningham C-4R competition roadster, drifting through a corner, tires clawing for grip, Hemi V-8 barking all the way. . . .

Throughout the 1960s, Chrysler performance went mostly in a straight line—and about a quarter mile at a time. Drag racing had matured considerably, the horsepower wars were raging between American manufacturers, and the muscle car era was in bloom. A second-generation Hemi came from the factory packing four-barrel carburetors and 426 cubic inches. Other notable MoPar performance motors included the 413 and 426 Wedges and the 440 Six-Pack, running three two-barrel

carbs. The nameplates these engines powered have all become significant pieces of muscle-car history: Road Runner, Barracuda, 300, Super Bee, Charger, Challenger.

Beginning about 1973, big-inch performance went on hiatus, at Chrysler and everywhere else. Government safety and emissions regulations, unleaded fuel, the boondoggles that were called "gas crunches" and other factors all conspired to quiet the voice of factory performance machines. By the end of the decade, Chrysler had to contend with all of the above, plus crippling financial woes that nearly put it out of business. Then along came Lido A. Iacocca.

Iacocca was among the senior managers who contributed to Ford's success in the 1960s. After being fired by Henry Ford II, he took over the top spot at Chrysler and was tagged as the man who could save the car maker from the bankruptcy looming over its head in the late 1970s. With a $1.5 billion loan guarantee from the U.S. government, a new management team, some new products (most notably the front-wheel-drive, modestly priced K-Car lines) and a lot of hard work, Chrysler turned itself around and stayed in business. It was also during Iacocca's term as chairman that one of the Viper's key creators joined Chrysler: Robert A. Lutz.

Bob Lutz is a "car guy" of the first order, having been with General Motors, Opel, BMW, and Ford of Europe. He joined Chrysler in 1986 and in January 1991 was appointed president of Chrysler Corporation, the position he holds as of this writing. You'll read much more about Mr. Lutz in later chapters.

The Izod concept car of 1985 may serve as a bit of a link in between the Cunninghams of the 1950s and the

Vipers of the 1990s. Though it shows virtually no resemblance to the Viper, it was conceived as a front-engined, V-8–powered roadster, though it never got beyond the mockup stage.

Besides the Cunningham, the Viper's two most obvious progenitors would have to be the Corvette and Shelby's 427 Cobra. The fiberglass Chevy two-seater had been making sales—and image—hay for GM for the better part of 40 years, a fact not lost on Chrysler management. While the 'Vette can be packaged for brute force or reasonable comfort, no such thing can be said of the Cobra. Its performance ability and legend need no introduction here: Its brute force would prove to be a key to the design philosophy of the Viper.

When Bob Lutz assembled the Viper's "Fourfathers" (himself included), he chose three other men whom he felt had the skills and the mind-set required to deliver the goods. The car needed to be conceived,

designed, engineered, built, and marketed in a unique fashion. For conceptual inspiration, he tapped on the shoulder of Carroll Shelby himself. What better way to ensure those Cobra vibes made it to Chrysler's no-nonsense roadster? The Shelby-Chrysler connection already existed, due to Carroll's role as a performance consultant to the company. The goal of Chrysler's design chief Tom Gale was to deliver eye-searing looks and packaging. To get the Viper from drawing board (and design computer) to the showroom required the drive of Chrysler's top engineering executive, Francois Castaing. Besides being savvy businessmen, these individuals are all serious automobile enthusiasts. Shelby's racing success needs no further explanation, and Castaing was involved with Renault's Formula 1 engine program. Gale and Lutz each have a stable of performance-oriented machinery.

According to both Shelby and Gale, Bob Lutz was really the "spark plug" behind the Viper concept:

Though this original concept vehicle shares no body panels with a production Viper, it's little short of amazing that so much of the look made the translation from show car to customer's garage; often by the time a dazzling concept car sees production, its impact is watered down considerably. *Chrysler*

The interior of the show concept car shares no detail with the production version, though a considerable amount of the shape and flavor did carry over. This car carries a five-speed transmission. *Matt Stone*

Shelby's Cobras, the Viper's most recent forebears. A black 427 follows an earlier 289-powered car. *Matt Stone*

build a modern-day Cobra using 1990s technology and design, with emphasis on performance above all else, yet make it producible by a large corporation, and deliverable for a well-below-six-figure price. No technology-laden gimmicks, not even ABS, just an elementally designed roadster with a huge naturally aspirated engine putting the power down to the rear wheels. A pure connection between machine, driver, and the road. Driving for the pure pleasure of it. As a marketing tool, such a machine could also do wonders for Chrysler's flagging performance image at the time (1988).

The VM01 vehicle of 1989 lacks sports bar, so the high-mounted stop light is mounted on the rear deck, as is the gas filler. As this machine does not have Viper-trademark sidepipes, the exhaust exits below the rear bumper. *Matt Stone*

Based upon very little more than a few conversations, Gale's Highland Park Advanced Design staff began sketching the shape that would become the Viper. Even the earliest renderings put all the right cues in the mix: an open roadster form, long hood, short deck, arching fenders and wheelwells over huge rolling stock. Windows? Door handles? A top? Forget 'em. This was to be a serious performance roadster. The Cobra cues were there, yet the look was not then, and is not now, just a restyled or updated version of the Cobra.

The heart and soul of any such automobile is the engine. While it would have been easy to understand if the design team just spec'd out an updated version of the 426 Hemi, they ultimately found their powerplant under the

NEXT
The VM01 and VM02 prototypes. VM01, foreground, was wearing what appeared to be production-based wheels when this photo was taken, but was often seen with different wheels. Note that all body panels are pinned in place and the lack of a "sports bar" and sidepipes. VM02 is a bit closer to production spec, though it wears aftermarket modular wheels. *Matt Stone*

The interior of VM-01 is business only, at best, as this vehicle's primary purpose was chassis and running-gear engineering. *Matt Stone*

LEFT
The dash plaque on VM01. It is interesting to compare this test mule to a production Viper. Though the basic shape is certainly familiar, there isn't a single exterior component that wasn't changed during the development process. *Matt Stone*

hood of a future *pickup truck.* According to Francois Castaing, "One of the first major projects we got going was to put a new big V-10 on its way. Jokingly, we said 'That's the kind of engine that back in the '60s, [Giotto] Bizzarrini and [Alejandro] DeTomaso would have bought to create the great sports car of back then. You know, very powerful, torquey, big gas American engine, put into a nice body.'" Dodge's new 8.0-liter (488-cubic-inch) V-10 was to be an all-iron unit, too heavy for the roadster project, but if it

BOB LUTZ, PRESIDENT, CHRYSLER CORPORATION

Chrysler President and Chief Operating Officer Bob Lutz. *Matt Stone*

Bob Lutz is a rabid automotive enthusiast who just happens to be the president and chief operating officer of Chrysler. He spent time with BMW and Ford of Europe prior to joining the company in 1986. Among his other passions are aircraft, motorcycles, and fine cigars! Bob is a Viper owner and spoke candidly about what the car means to the company and its customers.

Author: Chrysler has proven its ability to address enthusiast-market niches with Viper and concepts such as Prowler. How do you see Viper's success spilling over to other niches in the marketplace?

Lutz: Obviously, Viper has sent a strong signal [within] the corporation that it is a good thing to go with strong hunches, and if you have a clear vision on something that a small group of enthusiasts within the company would gladly and eagerly build for themselves, then you know that unless you're on a completely different planet, you know that if you do that vehicle, you're going to find a few thousand like-minded people per year [to purchase them]. That's really the philosophy that the Viper is all about, which is, dare to do something really terrific; not only despite the fact that nobody has tried it before, but because of the fact that nobody has tried it before.

Author: The GTS-R says a lot about Chrysler's enthusiasm for performance. In addition to producing the customer cars, do you envision a "works" GTS-R?

Lutz: None yet . . . It's not currently planned, but I wouldn't categorically say we would never do it.

Author: How different will the Viper of say, 2001 or 2005, be from today's?

Lutz: It will be evolutionary. The car will get better and better. By the 2001 it will be highly likely that the shape will not have changed at all, but we'll unquestionably go for ever more performance enhancements. We want to keep it the ultimate affordable sports car.

Author: So the shape and flavor could easily go ten years from the first production model?

Lutz: Sure. It can and will be something akin to the Porsche 911 . . . in its latest iteration, with still essentially the same shape, and yet the latest all-wheel-drive turbo [models] are thoroughly modern cars, and nobody looks at it as being an old vehicle.

Author: What would you change?

Lutz: I don't think I would change anything . . . I suppose if we could wave the magic wand, and were not dealing with such onerous noise restrictions, which pretty much dictate what you do about exhaust sound, we are always enthralled with the way they sound when we use low-restriction mufflers . . . you wish you had more sound and better sound, but it's hard to get there working around the ever-more-severe noise restrictions.

The VM-02 prototype. Much more of the Viper's final form is evident here when compared to VM-01. *Matt Stone*

could be cast in aluminum alloy and tuned for more horsepower . . . Shelby would later say that he initially favored the use of a large V-8, but according to many quotes from the other three "Fourfathers," it was "V-10 all the way."

With the major design elements in place, Lutz authorized construction of show and test vehicles in May 1988, with an eye toward the 1989 auto-show circuit. When the brilliant-red Viper show prototype was debuted at the 1989 North American International Auto Show in Detroit, not even the Chrysler managers could anticipate the response. The car appeared in newspapers and in every enthusiast magazine. There was a deluge of mail, phone calls, and even deposit checks. It was immediately apparent that Chrysler had a potential hit on its hands, and had to at least study the factors involved in actually producing it. Less than three months after the red roadster's appearance at Detroit, and a bit of discussion about hiring outside entities to build it, Chrysler announced the birth of Team Viper. This would be no everyday product, so there could be no ordinary way of designing and building it. Castaing chose Roy H. Sjoberg, who had joined Chrysler in 1985 after more than 20 years with GM, to assemble the team that would transform the show concept to production reality.

Cross-functional teams are not new to the industry, but the Viper would be the first Chrysler project designed and produced in this format (see sidebar). Instead of a project being passed from department to department, each member (design, production, purchasing, even suppliers) would be involved—and empowered—from the beginning, resulting in less waste, less time spent, and hopefully a more unified vision as to what the end result should be. The concept has proven highly successful, with Chrysler and many other auto manufacturers now developing products in this fashion.

The interior of VM-02 shows the wear and tear that comes from a hard life of engineering tests. *Matt Stone*

Space limitations do not allow us to cover every aspect of the Viper's preproduction development, and more details about hardware and actual performance will come in Chapter 2, but suffice it to say that in May 1990, 15 months after that first auto-show appearance, Chrysler announced that the Viper would be produced in limited quantity, with the first cars to be 1992 models. Viper was on the road to being on the road, so to speak.

And how did the car get its name? With the Cobra as its spiritual predecessor, a "snake" moniker was obvious. According to a quote from Bob Lutz in *Viper: Pure Performance by Dodge*, it came to him on an airplane trip. He toyed with names such as Python and Sidewinder, but none had the right ring. "So 'Viper' seemed to be . . . it rolls off of the tongue easily."

So it does.

Chapter Two

ON THE ROAD

"The challenge in the
development of Viper
was to go from concept to
production in less
than three years."
—*Francois Castaing*

It was clear that Viper would be no ordinary vehicle, even among performance cars, so special development and construction methods and a special group of people would be necessary to build it. Roy Sjoberg and other Chrysler managers interviewed hundreds of potential Team Viper members before selecting what they felt would be the most enthusiastic and qualified group. Its structure is much like that of a small entrepreneurial business, or perhaps a racing team, where problems are addressed immediately and solved quickly. There would

Yellow was added to the Viper palette in 1994. This is a 1995 RT/10, the last year for yellow (and dark green) Vipers. Both colors have been popular alternatives to the more common black or red. *Matt Stone*

This David Kimball cutaway of a 1992 Dodge Viper RT/10 shows the car's modern design and complexity. *Chrysler*

be an increased level of interaction between management and the people who actually assemble the product. Each "craftsperson" would have a much higher level of responsibility for a car's assembly than in the past, and often they would be involved in the build-up and installation of entire systems, rather than just attaching one component to each car as it rolls down a fast moving assembly line. Unlike in many production-line environments, Team Viper members also have direct communication with designers and engineers, so process improvement can be effected quickly. Groups of approximately five people assemble each Viper, one car at a time, in more of a true "custom-built" manner.

Chrysler selected its New Mack Avenue assembly plant in Detroit to be the home of Viper production. The plant was remodeled into a modern facility, yet one that would not be focused on high-speed car production, but rather hand assembly and the craftsmanship required to build low-production, niche-market vehicles.

The development of mainstream products often involves dozens, or even hundreds, of engineering mockups, prototypes, chassis "mules," and test vehicles. Team Viper, operating on both a strict budget and fairly short time constraints, did the job with only a few. Besides the original show vehicle, there were only a handful of engineering prototypes, plus a minimum of preproduction pilot vehicles.

The first prototype, chassis number VM01, was completed in December 1989 at a shop facility borrowed (commandeered would probably be a more accurate term) from Jeep, lovingly called "The Snake Pit." Painted white, it carried hand laid up fiberglass panels that were pinned to the frame and no rear "sport bar." Visually, it resembles the ultimate production Viper only in terms of overall shape and proportion. For power, it used a hopped-up Chrysler 360 V-8 and a German-made Getrag six-speed transmission.

The second prototype, chassis number VM02, was completed in April 1990. Painted red, this was the first Viper test mule to carry a V-10 engine, though it was an all-cast-iron unit, rated at 380 horsepower. A Borg-Warner six-speed trans replaced the Getrag unit, and a good deal of the Viper's production development was done on this vehicle. Still hand-built of fiberglass, it was also much of the media's first taste of a running Viper, as it appeared in many magazine articles.

The original steel-bodied show car was also a steel-bodied prototype built outside of Team Viper's Snake Pit, done by Metalcrafters in Southern California. Metalcrafters is a European-style carrozzeria that has developed numerous special projects and concept cars for Chrysler and other manufacturers.

The Viper's design and construction methods are a unique blend of time-tested, traditional elements, combined with very modern componentry and materials.

The philosophy was tightly focused on an elementally conceived brute of a roadster, yet everyone at Chrysler knew they would be heavily criticized if they ended up with too much of a throwback, or anything that could be written of as merely a factory-built "kit car."

Team Viper engineers chose tubular steel as the base material for the chassis. The steel space frame includes a center spine structure with tubular outriggers to support the body panels. This method of construction was selected over a monocoque for two reasons: to reduce development time over that of a stamped-steel, stressed-panel design and because monocoque designs rely on the roof structure to stiffen the overall chassis; but the Viper would have no roof. The Viper's chassis stiffness is exceptional for an open car, at approximately 5,000 pounds per degree of twist.

The suspension is fully independent, with unequal-length upper and lower control arms at each corner. With the exception of the front upper control arms, these pieces are fabricated from tubular steel. Two stabilizing toe links are used with the rear lower control arms, and gas-charged Koni coil-over shock/spring units with front and rear antiroll bars summarize the underpinnings. A car that is designed to hit well over 160 miles per hour needs powerful, fade resistant brakes, and the Viper has them: 13-inch ventilated discs with Brembo calipers at all four corners. ABS? Never was a part of the mix.

A unique three-spoke wheel design would carry Viper through its first four model years. Cast in aluminum alloy, the wheels measure 17x10 inches in front and 17x13 inches in the rear. Michelin developed special XGTZ unidirectional radials just for the Viper, size P275/40ZR17 and P335/35ZR17, respectively—the same steamroller-like

No multiple camshafts, four valves per cylinder, or other "exotica" for the Viper powerplant, just conventional V-8 technology brought up to modern standards . . . with two more cylinders, of course. Cutaway drawing by David Kimball. *Chrysler*

Like the Model T, the Viper was initially offered in but one color combination: red with a gray/black interior. More colors would soon follow. *Chrysler*

sizes found on the $250,000 Lamborghini Diablo. The rolling stock is controlled via power-assisted rack-and-pinion steering designed to provide maximum driver feedback and road feel, yet make the car easy to maneuver at very low speeds.

As mentioned, Team Viper had to get the car to production quickly, and on a budget. This all but ruled out tooling up for full steel body panels. Instead, a body and interior structure of several different resin transfer molding (RTM) composites was employed. Only the floorpan enclosure was formed of molded sheet steel. Besides the cost and time savings, the RTM panels yielded weight savings. "There's roughly about a one-third weight reduction of sheet metal," according to Roy Sjoberg.

In the RTM process, glass fibers are placed inside a mold, and once the mold is closed, resin is injected to mix with the fiberglass and form a finished panel. "We . . . control the panel-forming process so precisely that when each piece comes out of the mold, it will require only 10 to 15 minutes of hand finishing before reaching a 'Class A' level appearance," according to Russell Spencer, Viper technology development executive. This construction method will also likely aid the ease of future appearance updates.

What could be a more important part of a performance sports car than its engine? It is in this area that Chrysler went for a mix of pure big-block tradition and modern technology. Though there must have

VIPER AT LE MANS

It's interesting that a French company would sponsor this most American muscle car in the world's most important endurance race, but the Vipers proved both popular and capable at LeMans. This car finished 18th overall, and with more development, there is potential for a GT-class win. *Peter Brock*

The 24 Hours of Le Mans remains the ultimate test of a race car, its drivers, and its team. History has been made there, and people have died there. A recent reintroduction of GT classes has opened the door for entries like the Viper, and oddly enough, it was a French team that was first to build one for Le Mans. LMGT-1 class rules provide for few modifications, and the Rent A Car race team's two Vipers were amazingly stock. The cars ran hardtops and performed well considering the Viper's lack of racing development at the time. Intermittent transmission overheating and other niggling problems prevented a class win, but the cars finished 12th and 18th overall. The red #40 car's 12th place run, courtesy of Bertrand Balas, Justin Bell, and former F1 ace Rene Arnoux, was also good enough for a 3rd place in class.

When are more Vipers likely to compete on an international basis? See chapter 4.

Something missing from the picture? How about door handles! Harking back to sports cars of the past, Viper roadsters have no side windows or exterior door handles. To enter the car, you must open the door from the inside. *Chrysler*

been certain temptations to power the Viper with a modern-day rendition of the 426 Hemi or 440 Six Pack, in truth the car was destined for the V-10 virtually from the beginning. The earliest designs were built around it, and it is one of the features that gives the Viper its own identity, rather than that of a re-do of the Cobra or Cunningham.

As we know, the basis for the 8.0-liter "Copperhead" V-10 was the powerplant being developed for the new-for-'94 Dodge trucks. But the truck engine's power characteristics would be all wrong for a sports car and the all-iron construction too heavy. "I guess you could say we took a straight-forward approach in developing this engine," recalls Jim Royer, Team Viper engine manager. "We didn't

35

An imposing sight in anyone's rear view mirror, the Viper crossbar grille theme has now been translated throughout Dodge's product line, even to the Ram trucks and vans, a successful effort on Dodge's part to unify the appearance of its product line-up, and enjoy a bit of the performance-image rub-off from the Viper. *Chrysler*

The second color to be made available on the Viper, in 1993, was black. It has proven to be a very popular choice among purchasers. *Chrysler*

want to risk getting into exotic technology in so short a span . . . of development time."

Team Viper tapped the expertise of Lamborghini Engineering, which certainly had experience with high-performance street engines and would later develop V-10 engines for use in Formula 1 racing, though those engines were completely different units from those that

This tan and black interior scheme
was added for the 1994 model
year; it adds a touch of warmth
and looks particularly attractive on
an emerald green car. *Matt Stone*

would end up in the Viper. It
also probably helped that
Lamborghini was a Chrysler-
owned concern at the time.

The first goal was to
reduce the Viper engine's
weight versus the truck unit's
by at least 100 pounds. This
was accomplished by casting
both block and heads in aluminum. In keeping with muscle car tradition, the V-10
would retain its overhead-
valve configuration, with a single block-mounted camshaft.
The block, with six crankshaft
main bearings, employs an
interesting cooling strategy in
that an external water manifold running along the side of
the block provides coolant to
individual cylinders; it then
flows into the heads and back
to the radiator. The alloy cylinders contain iron liners and
forged alloy pistons, in the best
race-car tradition; compression
is a relatively low 9.1: 1.

VIPER PACES INDY

This hastily assembled prototype paced the 75th running of the Indianapolis 500 with Carroll Shelby at the wheel. It required virtually no modifications over stock to meet the Speedway's performance requirements. *Chrysler*

Dodge was in a bind. It had wanted to promote its new Stealth, and swung a deal with the Indianapolis Motor Speedway for the performance coupe to pace the 1991 500-mile race. One rub: the Stealth was built for Dodge by Mitsubishi, along with Mitsu's own quite similar 3000 model. When the word got out that what is essentially a Japanese car was scheduled to pace the Greatest Spectacle in Racing, a rumble of protest was issued forth from American enthusiasts. The fix? How about the new-for-1992 Dodge Viper?

Another problem: Team Viper was not yet ready to build production cars, much less one that would be showcased in front of more than 20 million race fans. As usual, they rose to the challenge, hand-building an essentially production-spec Viper prototype capable of exceeding the Speedway's performance criteria . . . in less than three months' time.

More than 1,800 miles of testing proved the car race-day ready, and two cars were actually prepared for pace-car duty. On May 26, 1991, racing legend and Viper patriarch Carroll Shelby paced Rick Mears' victory in the 75th Anniversary Indianapolis 500. It was Rick's fourth win, and also a big win for Team Viper. What began as a marketing and PR nightmare turned into a dream ride for this most American machine.

Custom-cast calipers, provided by Brembo of Italy, carry the Viper script and clamp huge ventilated rotors; ABS is not available and not really needed. Three-spoke wheels are a controversial element of the Viper's design; people seem to "love 'em or hate 'em." *David W. Newhardt*

An overhead view of the Viper V-10. Intake runners maximize "cross-ram" effect, but routing of throttle cables might have been neater. The front-hinging hood makes the most of the imposing engine's appearance and improves service access. Note the central location of the alternator. *David W. Newhardt*

Though dual Carter AFB four-barrel carbs would not seem out of place atop the Viper engine, it's hard to beat modern hardware when it comes to intake systems and engine management. An aluminum ram-tuned manifold system with dual plenums works in concert with multipoint fuel injection to deliver a docile idle and the low emission numbers that the old Hemi could only dream of. Thin-wall, cast exhaust manifolds each expel the spent gases via a one-piece stainless steel catalytic converter/muf-

Black-on-white gauges add a bit of a retro touch. Instrument visibility is excellent overall, as is performance from the heating and air conditioning system. Though it may seem a bit odd, one of the most pleasurable Viper driving modes is on a hot day with no top . . . and the AC on full blast! *David W. Newhardt*

Viper's imposing V-10 engine on display. The original concept show car can be seen in the rear. *Matt Stone*

fler combination housed in what may be one of the Viper's most interesting performance policy statements: those dual rocker-panel sidepipes, replete with labels warning "Hot Exhaust Pipe Below Door Opening" on the door sills. A fully electronic, distributorless ignition system works as part of a sophisticated engine-management computer system for maximum efficiency.

Every capacity of the Viper V-10 is "supersized": At 488 cubic inches, it's the largest mainstream production performance powerplant in the world. Its official

43

Sidepipes have singed more than a few legs, but as George Hamilton will attest, who cares about a little fried skin when you look so good? *David W. Newhardt*

On the original Viper show prototype, the chrome exhaust headers could be clearly seen through the reveal between the front fenders and the leading edge of the doors. Such a feature would never pass today's safety requirements, but the stylists preserved the look. The opening also serves to vent heat from the engine compartment. *David W. Newhardt*

The Viper logo pops up everywhere. Here it's embossed on the hood liner. *David W. Newhardt*

power rating (through 1995) was an even 400 horsepower at 4,600 rpm, with 450 pounds-feet of torque at 3,600 rpm. Oil capacity? Not 5 quarts . . . how 'bout 11! Nearly 4 gallons of coolant! The 6,000-rpm redline may sound conservative when compared to high-winding Ferrari and Porsche powerplants, but it's plenty high for an engine this large, and with so much torque on tap, more revs would serve little purpose. As a friend of mine, who is a big-block engine fanatic to an extreme, said of the Viper V-10: "Now that's a *motor*."

Backing the husky powerplant is a Borg-Warner Model T-56 six-speed manual transmission, simply one of the best manual transmissions available. Its quick shifting action and capable synchromesh

NEXT
This schematic outlines the Viper assembly process, from the build-up of the initial frame to the installation of the front fascia and final assembly prep. This is the process as it was at the New Mack Avenue plant for 1992–95 Vipers. *Chrysler*

NEW MACK AVENUE

FINAL ASSEMBLY

ROLL TEST

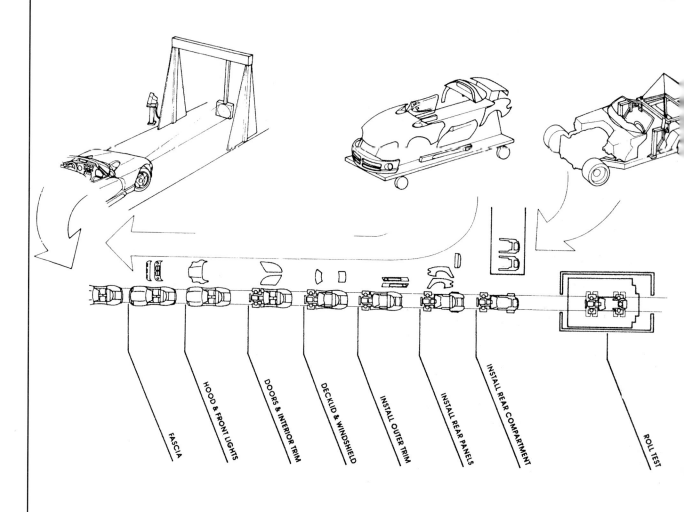

FASCIA

HOOD & FRONT LIGHTS

DOORS & INTERIOR TRIM

DECKLID & WINDSHIELD

INSTALL OUTER TRIM

INSTALL REAR PANELS

INSTALL REAR COMPARTMENT

ROLL TEST

ER ASSEMBLY PLANT

CHASSIS ASSEMBLY

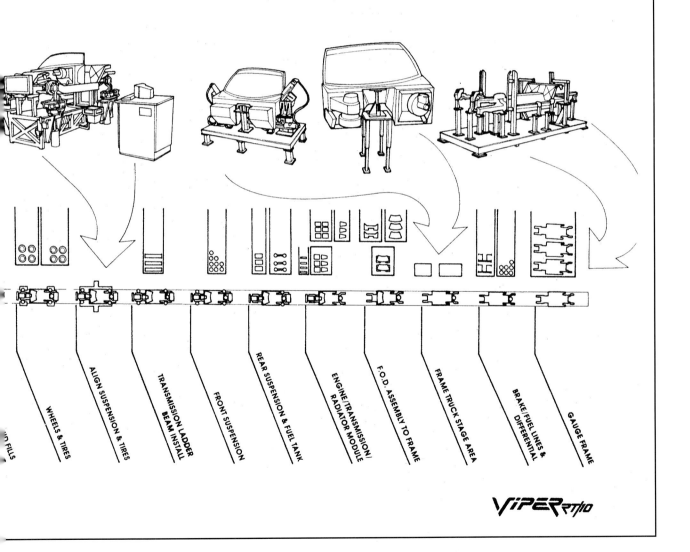

WHEELS & TIRES

ALIGN SUSPENSION & TIRES

TRANSMISSION LADDER
BEAM INSTALL

FRONT SUSPENSION

REAR SUSPENSION & FUEL TANK

ENGINE/TRANSMISSION/
RADIATOR MODULE

F.O.D. ASSEMBLY TO FRAME

FRAME TRUCK STAGE AREA

BRAKE/FUEL LINES &
DIFFERENTIAL

GAUGE FRAME

VIPER RT/10

"Tonight Show" host Jay Leno owns an eclectic collection of cars and motorcycles from Bugattis to Harley-Davidsons . . . and this 1994 Viper. Other celebrity owners include Tom Cruise and "Frasier" star Kelsey Grammer, the latter who received his yellow RT/10 as a gift from NBC to honor the show's Grammy-winning success. The top on Jay's Viper was custom made and has a smooth shape instead of the more commonly seen "double bubble." *David W. Newhardt*

Plant Manager Howard Lewis presents the keys to new Viper owner Wesley Wells, union president of IUE Local 775. The photo was taken at the New Mack Avenue Viper assembly plant. Wells also uses the vehicle as part of the union's effort to promote Chrysler products and a Chrysler technology lecture series. *Chrysler*

complement the engine perfectly. The transmission case is also cast in aluminum, and it connects to the V-10 via a 12-inch single-dry-disc clutch. The 3.07:1 final drive incorporates a limited-slip differential.

The cockpit is quite traditional, focusing on driver input and performance: Luxury seekers should look elsewhere. Comfortable, well-bol-stered leather seats are separated by a fairly wide console. As the driver grips the three-spoke, leather-wrapped steering wheel, the speedometer/odometer, tachometer, and warning-light cluster are in plain view. Ancillary gauges (oil pressure, voltage, coolant temp, and fuel level) are in a binnacle at the top of the console, which also houses the

Performance Comparison
Source: *Car and Driver*, July 1995

Model	0–60 (sec)	0–100 (sec)	1/4-Mile (ET/speed)	Top Speed (mph)	Price (as tested)
Viper RT/10	4.3	10.5	12.8@109	168	$61,975
Ferrari F355	4.5	10.9	13.0@110	179	$128,800
Acura NSX-T	5.2	13.0	13.8@103	162	$86,642
Lotus Esprit S4S	4.4	10.9	13.0@108	162	$87,904
Porsche 911 Turbo	3.7	9.4	12.3@114	175	$106,465

Chrysler/Alpine sound system and heating, ventilation, and air conditioning (HVAC) controls. A security system is standard.

If anything speaks to the Viper's true purpose, yet seems to draw criticism, it is the first roadster's weather protection systems . . . or lack of same. Roll-up windows? None. Exterior door handles? *Nada*. Hard top? Zip. In their place, Chrysler designed a cloth top with zip-in side-curtain windows that do enclose the car, but would have to be considered vestigial at best. They're not particularly handsome and make the Viper feel a bit claustrophobic inside. When stowed, these pieces eat up a majority of the none-too-commodious trunk space. But hey, if you want to drive in a cocoon, you're looking at the wrong car!

The press, and the buying public, went bonkers for the Viper. Dodge had generated an overwhelming amount of PR, brand identity, and showroom traffic with the car. Every major automotive magazine has had a Viper on its cover; some several times in the same year! Even today, a Viper on the road turns heads; one parked at the side of the road instantaneously draws a crowd.

It's also interesting that this most American of roadsters would also be sold abroad. Export Vipers (badged as Chryslers, not Dodges) have an exhaust system that exits out the back of the car through large dual chrome pipes, metric gauges, revised lighting systems, tow hooks, wider license-plate brackets, and numerous other changes required to make it conform to the varying regulations of European countries. One thing doesn't change: Vipers are as much of a hit in Paris or Frankfurt as they are in Los Angeles or Cleveland.

It would be impossible to summarize the considerable media reaction, but even a sampling of the commentary is worth note. *Car and Driver*'s Kevin Smith wrote, ". . . Viper is one of the most exciting rides since Ben Hur discovered the chariot . . . It's intended to go fast, stop hard, hang onto corners and give everyone in sight—driver, passenger, and bystanders—a thrill that will make their day." I particularly enjoy *Sports Car International* editor Jay Lamm's thoughts: "The Viper is about having fun, playing games, and reliving a great childhood—maybe even somebody else's—and it's almost cheap enough for people to believe they could have one themselves someday, given a lot of hard work or a little good luck. It's an inclusionary sort of dream machine."

Ron Sessions of *Road & Track* reveled in his first Viper driving experience: ". . . a driving route that included freeway cruising, delicious cut-and-thrust

Many feel the Viper is most handsome in profile; as curvaceous as the car is, it also has many fairly flat surfaces. The sport bar, besides providing an anchor for the folding top and a mounting spot for the center, high-mounted stop light, does a lot to visually break up the large planes of the Viper's hood and deck. *Chrysler*

twisty bits, wicked mountain switchbacks, wide-open stretches of high desert and some apex clipping hot laps at Willow Springs Raceway has afforded me a full measure of quality man-meets-machines bonding time. And with a tangled nest of split ends that passes for hair, I have the Viper-doo to prove it. . . ." It would be hard to gather the impact of Viper's first four model years into one short paragraph, but *Motor Trend* came close when it said, "Nothing you can drive packs the personality, makes the statement, or snaps your neck like the Dodge Viper RT/10. Nothing at all." The stuff that legends are made of.

CHAPTER THREE

VIPER VARIATIONS

*"...it felt like this car had some
Cobra ancestry or
something. The flexibility of it
is unbelievable. It's got bags of
torque everywhere"*
—Phil Hill, on the Hennessey
Viper Venom 550

The amount of enthusiasm generated by the Viper is akin to dropping a very large rock in the middle of a pond: a significant ripple effect was bound to follow. Chrysler gained new understanding of the value of the "team approach" to designing and building cars. It also proved to the world, the car industry, and to *itself* that a large multinational corporation can develop products for niche markets. As discussed, Viper also drew an amazing amount of media reaction. It's only natural, then, to

On the track in a Skip Barber Driving School Viper. Vipers provide an opportunity for students to drive a very high-performance vehicle with the instructor as passenger/observer, something that can't be done in a single-seat, open-wheel machine. *Skip Barber Driving School*

The Ram VTS prototype carries as many Viper cues as would translate from roadster to pickup truck, including a special front fascia with fog lights and Viper GTS prototype wheels. *Chrysler*

expect Viper's influence to extend to other Chrysler products, the aftermarket, and to the fertile imagination of the buying public.

Dodge Ram VTS

Trucks are big business. In fact, the best-selling vehicle in America has been the Ford F-150 for many years running. And modified, personalized, downright *hot-rodded* trucks are a big part of the picture. So in 1994, with Dodge bringing out its first all-new pickup in more than 20 years—with the first-ever production V-10 engine—the Ram VTS concept vehicle is almost no surprise. The Ram's iron V-10 produces 300 horsepower and 450 pounds-feet of torque, and it's no secret that it and the Viper's all-alloy "Copperhead" V-10 began life on nearby

drawing boards. Dodge whipped up the VTS to have a little fun, and to gain a little press. "We knew it would only be a matter of time until someone would try to pack a Viper V-10 engine into a Ram truck," said Chrysler designer Mike Castiglione at the Ram VTS's unveiling. "We thought Dodge ought to beat them to the punch."

The VTS carries the Viper V-10 and six-speed transmission, as well as prototype future Viper wheels. The special front air dam includes Viper-style fog lights, and the paint scheme matches the Viper GTS Coupe. It was built off of a standard-cab Ram 1500 pickup.

Though the VTS drew both attention and admiration, Chrysler claims it never intends to put the truck into production. This is understandable, given that others had tried marketing factory high-performance trucks and had experienced only moderate success. GMC's Syclone of 1991, with a turbo V-6, was dropped after two years in production; the Chevrolet SS 454 lived only a bit longer. Ford's Special Vehicle Team fared much better with its fine handling Lightning, but elected to drop it after the 1995 model year. The VTS remains but a potent dream.

Plymouth Prowler

Hot-rodding has been experiencing a renaissance over the last decade, way up from an all-time low during the mid-1970s. Today's hot rods are often beautifully crafted, high-performance machines, and hot-rodding has also become a legit family sport, versus the outlaw image it had immediately after World War II. This fact was certainly not lost on Chrysler, and the result is the Prowler. Badged as a Plymouth to inject some spunk into that somewhat sagging name brand, the Prowler, like the Viper, was originally built to test the waters of market reaction. ". . . the Plymouth Prowler takes the traditional definition of a 'hot rod,' refines it for a '90s culture, and again demonstrates Chrysler's ability to define trends before they reach the surface," according to Chrysler's PR materials.

The Prowler eschews the typical hot-rod V-8 and the Viper's V-10; instead it has become a showcase for one of Chrysler's more mainstream engines, the 3.5-liter SOHC V-6. Originally introduced in the LH line of cars (Dodge Intrepid, Chrysler Concord, Eagle Vision) the V-6's stock rating of 214 horsepower gets uprated to 240 horses via a unique exhaust system. The Prowler also marks the first use of this engine in a rear-wheel-drive car, and it delivers power via a rear-mounted four-speed automatic transaxle and the Autostick shift control mechanism.

The all-aluminum bodywork is clearly flavored after a 1930s roadster, but one that's been updated to 1990s standard by one of hot-rodding's legendary builders such as John Buttera or Boyd Coddington. It was styled in-house by Tom Gale's staff, and neatly integrates the fenders into a basic body shape that appears fenderless. A stowaway coupe top is also part of the prototype package. The chassis is also all-aluminum; suspension is fully independent, and offers four-wheel disc brakes. At 165 inches, the Prowler is about 10 inches shorter than a Viper.

Interesting too is the use of 295/40R20 tires on the Prowler's rear axle, the first modern American OEM use of 20-inch-diameter tires and wheels on a production passenger car.

An all-alloy Viper V-10 replaces the iron V-10 in the Ram VTS. A Borg-Warner T-56 six-speed manual gearbox is also part of the swap. The conical air filter looks like a bit of an afterthought, but again this vehicle was never designed for serious production consideration. *Chrysler*

Chrysler took another step toward cementing its reputation as America's premier niche-vehicle builder by developing the Plymouth Prowler, set to come to market as a 1997 model. The neo hot rod goes new tech with an overhead-cam V-6 power and an automatic transaxle. Wonder if the Viper's V-10 would fit . . . *Chrysler*

Chrysler must have been serious about the Prowler, as the original concept vehicle was built to meet all passenger-car safety standards, including dual air bags and all required lighting. After much market and production feasibility study, Chrysler announced in January 1996 that the Prowler will be produced as a 1997 model, with pricing estimated in the mid-$30,000 range.

Skip Barber Driving School

Slightly modified sedans and detuned Formula Fords are common fare at many racing schools, but the Skip Barber curriculum includes Dodge Dakota V-8

pickups, Stealths, Stratuses, open-wheel Dodge-powered Formula cars . . . and Vipers. Barber opened his first racing school in 1975; all school cars are now Dodge or Dodge-powered vehicles, as of 1995. This marketing arrangement is similar to that of the Bob Bondurant School of High Performance Driving, which uses Ford product exclusively. Various Barber courses are offered at more than a dozen tracks around the country.

The Viper plays an important role at the Dodge/Skip Barber Driving School and is used primarily for autocross portions of the course. It allows the driver a chance to learn in a very high-perfor-

SHELBY VIPER RT/10 CS

Shelby cues are obvious on the RT/10 CS special-edition Viper. Grille bars are removed for more Cobra-esque frontal treatment, and the color scheme is an exact duplicate of that used so extensively on Shelby Cobras and GT 350 Mustangs. Too many Shelby signatures and logos hinder what is otherwise a very good look. *Visual Graphics*

It only figures that someone would attempt to forge the "missing link" between Carroll Shelby's original Cobras and the Viper. That someone is Dan Fitzgerald. Fitzgerald was one of Shelby's top-selling dealers back in the good old days, and his Fitzgerald Motorsports concern has come up with a special-edition Shelbyized Viper.

Visuals include a '65-Shelby spec Wimbledon white/ Guardsman blue paint scheme, modular wheels, a rear wing, hard top, and a revised grille opening more resembling that of a Cobra. The interior gets special seating and belts. The whole package is lathered in better than a dozen Shelby signature or "CS" logos, with the glove box lid hand-signed by Shelby, including a special serial number. It's not all show, as the package includes free-flow exhausts, a switch to 3.73:1 rear-end ratio, stiffer sway bar and shocks, and other performance tweaks.

It's a striking package, though some feel it carries more Shelby labels than are really needed. Anyone seeing those blue stripes over that white roadster shape is bound to know who was involved. Only 50 Shelby Viper RT/10 CSs are being built.

Toys, toys, toys. There is a plethora of "Viperbilia" available, even though the car has only been available for five years. *Scott Mead*

John Hennessey takes the Viper to the max, offering 500-plus-cubic-inch "stroker" versions rated at up to 600 horsepower. Though appearance modifications, like these Shelby-inspired "skunk stripes", are available, Hennessey concentrates his efforts on improving performance. While other shops offer turbo- or supercharging, Hennessey prefers to stick with more traditional upgrades to a naturally aspirated engine. All this speed doesn't come cheap, however. A 550-horsepower upgrade adds approximately $30,000 to the stock Viper's nearly $60,000 price tag. *Hennessey Motorsports*

European-based tuners are also getting into the Viper act. This Challenger R version was designed and built by Bernd Michalak of Mainz, Germany. Said to be a "race or road" version, it features a cut-down windshield, a single driver's roll hoop replacing the factory targa bar, and a revised air exhaust cutout at the base of the windshield. The headlight covers have been removed, and the fog-light openings appear to have been converted into cooling ducts. *Matt Stone collection*

mance vehicle, yet being a two-seater, an instructor can ride along to observe the student's technique, something not possible in a single seater. According to Rick Roso, the school's PR manager, the Vipers are "*very* popular" with students and teachers alike!

Viper Television Show

You need only look at the specially equipped Aston Martin DB5 driven by James Bond in *Goldfinger* and *Thunderball* to understand the impact that a starring role in a major movie or TV show can have on a car's reputation . . . and sales. Remember Martin Milner's Corvette in *Route 66*? Sales of black and gold Pontiac Trans Ams skyrocketed after the success of Burt Reynolds' *Smokey and the Bandit*. And so on.

When NBC not only selected the Viper (and several other Chrysler vehicles) to appear in its 1994 action-adventure series, and actually named the show *Viper*, it seemed to be a dream marketing vehicle (pun intended) for Dodge. "In a future where criminals outgun and outrun the law, one man and one machine will change all the rules," according to NBC PR materials. The show starred James McCaffery, Dorian Harewood, and Joe Nipote. McCaffery's character, Michael Payton, is a bad-guy-turned-good-guy who now takes out after his old gang, "The Outfit."

The Viper's bag of tricks makes most other show-time vehicles, such as the K.I.T.T. Firebird from *Knight Rider*, look tame. In off-duty guise, it appeared to be a standard red Viper. When it is time for action, the car "morphs" into the armored "Defender" Viper, a gray hardtop, replete with "fangs" in the grille. An advanced satellite system, tractor beams, and the like are employed as plot devices intended to render the villains' cars helpless.

Several standard Vipers, plus the Defender show car (styled by Neil Walling and crew as an official factory project), were employed in production. One had its entire front end removed to create a camera car, and at least two Vipers were fitted with 360-cubic-inch V-8 engines and automatic transmissions for stunt work. Though the show featured glossy sets and solid special effects work, the net result was a marginal effort at best. To quote one particular TV critic, It wasn't exactly *Masterpiece Theatre*. *Viper* was canceled after one season and 13 episodes.

The "Defender" Viper from the less-than-a-hit TV show, *Viper*. Still, it was great fun to watch a standard red Viper roadster "morph" into this car. The series sets and special effects were well done. The Defender was built by Metalcrafters. *Matt Stone*

Viperbilia

For a car that's been available for a little less than five years as of this writing, the amount of automobilia available to Viper fans is phenomenal. Metal die-cast models, plastic model kits, toys, and radio controlled Vipers are available from just about every major manu-facturer; die-cast manufacturer Burago reported its Viper

NEXT
Though the Viper was conceived as a performance sports car, it's hard to keep a hot Dodge off the drag strip. Vipers are a very popular sight at Saturday-night grudge races all across the country. Viper quarter-mile ETs sometimes approach the 10-second range. *David W. Newhardt*

SUMMARY OF MAJOR PRODUCT CHANGES
1992-1995

1992 Model Year
Original-specifications roadster; available only in red exterior color;
no air conditioning

1993 Model Year
Black exterior paint color added
Reverse lock-out feature added to transmission
Windshield antenna replaces mast antenna
Battery relocated to left frame rail
Front and rear bumpers now of composite material

1994 Model Year
Emerald green and bright yellow exterior paint colors added
Black and tan interior color scheme added
Factory-installed air conditioning available
Passenger-door grab handle added

1995 Model Year
New one-piece cast intake manifold

—Source, Chrysler

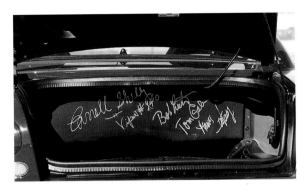

Most autograph seekers present a book, magazine, or photograph. Not Lou Nese, who presented his trunk to Viper "Fourfathers" Lutz, Shelby, Castaing, and Gale for their autographs. *Matt Stone*

models as its top seller for quite some time. A number of prints and posters are offered, some by Dodge Marketing, and the Viper appears to be giving the Lamborghini Countach a run for the top spot as car poster pin-up. Sportswear From Mopar offers several Viper clothing items, as do several aftermarket producers, and many unique collectibles are advertised in *Viper Quarterly* (see Additional Reading). Several firms have also begun to offer more boutique-quality items, often of the "signed and numbered" variety, such as plates, lithos, and the like.

A good place for the first-time purchaser to begin shopping for Viper items is Chrysler's own *Concept and Vintage* and *Viper Holiday Gift* catalogs, available from

Using cars in product ads is nothing new, but the Viper has quickly become a favorite advertising eye catcher. It's also sure to rival the Lamborghini Countach as a poster pin-up favorite. *Matt Stone*

Viper series star James McCaffery suits up to take a Viper cutaway camera car for a "ride." This rig is towed behind another vehicle for close-up moving shots; a big improvement over the old technique of a movie screen sitting behind the car. *NBC Publicity*

MIC (PO Box 877, Troy, MI, 48099). The catalog lists officially licensed die-casts, models, displays, and much more.

The Aftermarket

To quote Chrysler President Bob Lutz: "Power in the Viper is like your personal bank account. There's no such thing as too much of it." No matter how much performance and style a manufacturer builds into an automobile, there is an imaginative aftermarket industry waiting to offer parts and accessories intended to increase one or both elements. The Viper is no different. It's natural for enthusiasts to personalize their machines, especially with an automobile that was at first offered in only one body style—and in only one color!

Demand surfaced early for a hard top to replace the stock folding soft top, and several manufacturers offered them American Sunroof Corporation (ASC), long experienced in the top and sunroof business, offers one with sort of a "double-bubble" look, reminiscent of Zagato designs of the 1950s. TGF and Applied Racing Technologies also offer aftermarket hardtops, and Dodge offered its own factory-optional unit beginning with the 1996 model year.

One of the most common upgrades is the installation of aftermarket wheels. There are high-quality modular wheels available for the Viper, but it's important to stay close to the size and offset of the factory pieces, as fender clearance and wheel alignment are critical. Many owners have simply chosen to chrome or polish their stock wheels for a different look.

Every marque seems to attract its own top "tuner." For Mercedes, it's AMG. For the Viper, the top performance aftermarket vendor so far is Hennessey Motorsports. In barely four years time, John Hennessey and his staff have developed a worthy line-up of performance parts. Hennessey also assembles these parts in packages to create his Venom Vipers: the Venom 500, Venom 550, and now the Venom 600 replete with a "stroker" crankshaft that takes the V-10 out to 520 cubic inches. Hennessey's hopped-up Vipers have been tested by several enthusiast magazines, and have delivered startling accelera-

tion times. *Motor Trend*, for example, tested a Venom 550 for its July 1994 issue and achieved a 0–60 time of 3.5 seconds, with an elapsed time in the quarter mile of 11.7 seconds! The test also included a stock Viper that delivered 4.5 and 13.2 seconds, respectively.

The RT/10 engine responds well to Hennessey's fairly straightforward modifications. Revised throttle bodies, ported/polished intake manifolds and cylinder heads, and a "cold-air" system improve intake airflow; a less-restrictive stainless steel exhaust system reduces back pressure. An optional 3.73:1 rear end ratio further increases low-end response. Venom 550s pick up their additional horsepower with the addition of stainless steel headers, a revised camshaft, and further revisions to the valvetrain. Still more products are under development by Hennessey, and other shops have built turbocharged and supercharged Vipers.

Said Richard Meaden, in Britain's *Performance Car* magazine: "The Hennessy Viper Venom 550 is the closest thing to experiencing an off-shore power-boat on dry land." And *Motor Trend* summed up its review of Hennessey's steroidal snakes as follows: "The social deviates among our test staff agree: Too much horsepower is barely enough." Indeed.

Chapter Four

A NEW RT/10, THE GTS, AND BEYOND

"We want to keep it the ultimate
affordable sports car."

—Bob Lutz

Going forward, it appears that Viper—both the story and the product itself—will be an evolutionary entity. Team Viper makes a point of noting that it does not wait for model-year changeover time to imbue the car with the latest improved hardware. Though this may drive collectors and historians who track every little part number

Chrysler made plans for a first year run of approximately 1,700 GTS Coupes. More than 2/3 of that total were snapped up by existing RT/10 owners. MSRP for the 1996 GTS coupe is $66,700, a little less than $10,000 more than a roadster—plus gas guzzler and luxury taxes. Don't let the power windows and CD player fool you into believing the Viper has gone soft: The GTS features a substantially revised engine rated at 450 horsepower, only about 75 fewer ponies the base engine in the GTS-R racer. *Bill Delaney*

An early 1992 photograph of a Viper GTS Coupe styling study. This clay mockup used standard RT/10 sidepipes, which were not used on GTS prototypes, and standard Viper wheels. The "double-bubble" roofline was already a part of the mix. *Chrysler*

change and update a bit batty in the future, the buyer gets the benefit of having the most improved version available at the time. Still, the 1992–1995 RT/10 stands quite markedly as the "first-generation" Viper. Beginning in 1996, the pace picked up considerably, with a much-updated RT/10, production of the GTS coupe, and announcement of the GTS-R factory racer. The chronology is a bit interwoven, as the initial GTS coupe development began in 1992, the same year the RT/10 began series production.

Late 1992 concept drawings of the GTS Coupe. The sidepipes are capped off, and the rear-exiting exhaust is in place. *Chrysler*

As surely as cars like the Cunningham and 427 Cobra were the spiritual predecessors of the Viper RT/10, progenitors of those same eras—such as the Ferrari 250 GTO, the Shelby Daytona Cobra Coupe, and of course coupe versions of the Chrysler-powered Cunningham racers—appear to have inspired the Viper GTS Coupe.

The first GTS Coupes were shown at the North American Auto Show in Detroit and the Greater Los Angeles Auto Show in January 1993. Though billed as "An Automotive Concept" at the time, the crowd reaction was much the same as it was to the original Viper show car just a few years before: Build it! Shown in an arresting shade of metallic blue, sporting an exceptionally handsome chrome five-spoke alloy wheel design and race-inspired white "Cunningham stripes" down the middle of the hood,

Carroll Shelby and Francois Castaing answer questions during the Viper GTS Coupe press conference at the 1993 Greater Los Angeles Auto Show. *Matt Stone*

71

The striking "ketchup and mustard" color combo recalls Ferrari endurance racers of the 1960s. This 1996-only combination is the only Viper to date to include the snake logo on its fenders. *Matt Stone*

1996 Viper RT/10s, replete with new color combinations. The jury is still out on whether the two-tone paint and interior schemes will be popular or not. Some tradiationalists seem to prefer the purity of a single bold color, others like the contrast. *Chrysler*

top, and deck, the GTS looked for all the world to be an updated, streetable version of the aforementioned Daytona Cobra Coupe or Cunningham C4R-K. Only six Daytonas were built, all race cars, and they carried the Shelby team to the World Championship for Makes title in 1965.

I was with Peter Brock, Shelby American team member and designer of the Daytona Coupe, when the wraps first came off the GTS at that '93 LA Auto Show. Brock commented, "Tom Gale came to me with some of the original drawings of the GTS Coupe the previous August at the Pebble Beach Concours d'Elegance and asked my opinion of the new car. He wanted to make sure that I had no problem with the resemblance to the Daytona, especially the blue and white paint scheme.

The factory-offered hardtop and new-for-1996 sliding-glass side-window package are big improvements over the first-generation Viper's weather protection package. It looks better, is quieter, and lets in less water and air—and it can be retrofitted to 1992–95 Vipers. *Chrysler*

ROY H. SJOBERG, EXECUTIVE ENGINEER, VIPER PROJECT

Roy Sjoberg might as well be considered the Viper's "Fifthfather," if there were such a thing. He assembled the Team Viper members and facilitated the car's transition from concept, to show car, to production. Roy has an extensive background in the development and production of performance automobiles, including more than 20 years at General Motors.

Author: From an engineering and production standpoint, the Viper has been very evolutionary, even though it appears much the same. How many "tweaks" has it received since production began?

Sjoberg: Each engineering change could have 10 or 12 tweaks, so it's difficult to say, but for the most part, probably one-third of the product has changed, not including the 1996 models. It's a continuous improvement, a continuous evolution . . . why not give the customer, as soon as you can, the improved product?

Author: Do you envision an automatic transmission for the Viper?

Sjoberg: No. We've not seen a great demand from our buyers, and we feel it's contrary to the basic image of the vehicle.

Author: When does Job #1 [the first 1996 Viper] roll out of the new Viper plant?

Sjoberg: Job #1 rolls out in roughly one week [mid-October, 1995]! We're in the process of getting ready. The new plant has moved along very, very well, and we always said we would introduce in the September/October [1995] time frame, always thinking it would be later than earlier. The facility is moving along very rapidly.

Author: Do you happen to recall the relative weight comparisons for this body material versus steel or aluminum, and for what other reasons did you choose polypropylene and fiberglass type materials?

Sjoberg: We did some comparisons, and it's difficult to remember [the exact numbers] off the top of my head, but roughly there's about a one-third weight reduction over sheet metal. The real reason for selecting the material was not only reduction, but lower investment. When you talk about metal forming . . . you are talking about substantial dies and substantial facility investments.

Author: So you saved considerable cost?

Sjoberg: Yes; [we saved] time to market and tooling investment. That's correct.

Author: What would you most like to change about the Viper?

Sjoberg: I think we're addressing it. I really have no compelling drive in the back of my cranium that says, "We've gotta do this, and we've gotta do it quickly." We are about to do the coupe that I believe will provide our customer with [the car] they'd like to see in the next evolution.

The 1996 Viper line-up, as shown at the famous Pebble Beach Lodge in California, features a GTS Coupe Indy pace car and one of each color of the RT/10 roadster. *Matt Stone*

I was flattered that they would even consider asking my permission . . . Overall, it just pointed out what a class act Tom Gale was running with the Viper program."

Prototype GTS Coupes made the rounds among the automotive enthusiast magazines, and in 1994 Chrysler made the announcement that the Viper GTS Coupe would be a production reality for the middle of the 1996 model year. But making the GTS production-ready would take more work than just creating new fast-back bodywork, so its development was done in concert with a substantially updated roadster.

A 1996 hand-assembled prototype during a media test day at Willow Springs Raceway, Rosamond, California, November 1995. David W. Newhardt

Part of the tooling-up process for the coupe would involve a new home for all Viper production. In April 1995, Chrysler announced that the New Mack Avenue assembly plant would be remodeled for the production of a new generation of truck engines. By midyear, a 345,000-square-foot facility (on Conner Avenue in

ABOVE AND RIGHT
This Shelby-inspired color combination features white painted wheels and blue-accented interior. The colors are an exact match of those used on the original Shelby GT 350. The open grille area brings to mind the 427 Cobra's front end. *Matt Stone*

Detroit) had been acquired and established as the new Viper production facility for 1996 models and beyond.

RT/10 for 1996

The 1996 roadster will be a unique piece of Viper history, as it is really a bridge between the '92–'95 cars, and the '97-and-beyond models. This scenario is somewhat reminiscent of the 1968 Jaguar "Series 1-1/2" E-Type, which shared componentry with the multiyear run of cars before and after it. Because of the plant move and the completion of

GTS Coupe tooling, Dodge only made plans to produce about 600–700 '96 RT/10s.

Immediately noticeable is the switch from rocker-mounted sidepipes to a rear-exit exhaust system, with two large chrome pipes just below the license plate. This was seen on the first GTS concept car, and is very similar to the system on European-delivery Vipers. The exhaust pipes still follow along the sills, but now turn inboard forward of the rear wheels. The pipes then pass over the rear suspension and enter a tandem muffler. Some felt that the "five-per-side" exhaust sound of the original pipes left something to be desired; to this writer's ears, the new system is a vast improvement.

Three '96-only color schemes were introduced; no more emerald green or yellow Vipers, at least for now. The choices are black exterior with silver accents and a black interior, white with blue accents (more Shelby cues), or a combination quickly nicknamed "ketchup and mustard": red with bright yellow wheels and a yellow Viper logo just ahead of the front doors. Squint hard and this little yellow snake could just as easily be a little yellow prancing horse on the fender of a red Ferrari endurance racer! The white cars will also have blue leather accenting the steering wheel, shifter, and handbrake lever; the red/yellow combo includes red leather on the same interior pieces.

The five-spoke wheels that were such a hit on the GTS show cars became standard production pieces for 1996 RT/10s. They are silver on black cars, white for white models, and the aforementioned yellow on the red ones. All roadsters (and the GTS) got new rolling stock as well. Though the sizes

ABOVE AND LEFT
Separated at birth? Peter Brock penned the original Daytona Cobra Coupe nearly 30 years prior to the introduction of the GTS Coupe. Similarities are amazing. *Matt Stone and Chrysler*

remain the same, Michelin designed its new Pilot SX MXX3 tires for improved performance, wet or dry. They are also a bit lighter than the previous XGT Z tires.

If there's one thing the Viper needed, even for a hard-core roadster, it was improved weather protection, and a real top for when *al fresco* is not the preferred method of travel. Though several aftermarket companies offered hardtops almost immediately after introduction, Team Viper chose to offer a factory optional unit for 1996. It also fit the previous models. The previous zip-out plastic side curtains gave way to sliding glass units, which can be used with the hard top or the soft top. Much better.

Many of the '96-model improvements are found beneath the skin, such as a revised chassis that is even torsionally stiffer than the original. The new exhaust also reduces back pressure, so the power and

torque ratings increase to 415 horsepower and 488 pounds-feet, respectively. A power-steering cooler was added. Other driveline revisions included a new windage tray for the engine, a stronger differential that is more stiffly mounted to the chassis, and uprated drive shafts.

The big change to the suspension system involved cast-aluminum control arms and knuckles to replace the previous steel and cast-iron pieces. The change of material gives a weight reduction of approximately 60 pounds. The rear roll center was lowered slightly and the suspension geometry was revised to reduce changes during suspension travel; the rear caster angle was also revised. Pickup points for the suspension were relocated to increase the effective shock-absorber travel; higher-rate springs (18 percent rear, 12 percent front) and revised shock-absorber

This GTS Coupe concept vehicle still shows sidepipes with block-off caps; production versions will have revised rocker panels that still bulge out for pipe clearance, but the sidepipe openings will be gone. *Chrysler*

valving was specified. A recalibrated power-brake booster provides easier pedal modulation, as some owners and media road testers complained that the brakes were a bit too touchy.

All of the above work together to not only increase overall handling limits but to improve control as the Viper nears its handling limits. The car was often criticized as being too quick to "break away" at the limit of adhesion; having driven a preproduction '96 with the new suspension hardware and calibration, I can say it felt more progressive, communicative, and controllable than did the earlier Vipers—an improvement to what was already a fine-handling sports car.

GTS Coupe

As noted, the Viper GTS Coupe is far more than just a quick, hard-topped re-skin of the RT/10 roadster. Though the look is certainly Viper, there are numerous detail changes to the exterior—so many that it's really a different car. Also, Chrysler's marketing position for the GTS Coupe is much more luxury oriented than with the roadster.

The front fascia is a different unit, as are the driving lights, and of course the entire rear treatment was designed for the coupe. A race-inspired aluminum quick-fill gas cap sprouts from the passenger-side sail panel, and the top itself has two gentle bulges to improve head (or helmet?) room. Louvers sprouted along the crest of the front fenderline,

ABOVE AND BELOW

The Viper GTS-R's maiden voyage in competition was at the Rolex Daytona 24-hour enduro in February 1996. Though they showed class-leading speed during practice and qualifying, new-car teething problems prevented either from a top finish, though the #98 Dismore/Cobb/Archer/Hendricks car had run as high as third in class. Their performance at Sebring a month later was also problem plagued, but the team gathered on-track experience that simply cannot be gained in testing. Chrysler remains solidly committed to the GTS-R and has its sights firmly focused on the 24 Hours of Le Mans. GTS-R project partners such as Reynard, Brembo, and Borg-Warner all have considerable racing experience and success, and they provide Neil Hanneman's team the support needed to make the cars viable in the revitalized GT class. Canaska/Southwind Motorsports managed the Viper teams' efforts for these first two outings. *G. Hewitt*

NEXT

From this angle a bit of the "double bubble" aspect of the GTS Coupe's roofline is visible. This is a well-known styling cue, employed mostly by Italian styling house Zagato to provide additional headroom (or helmet room) in smaller sports cars. Several Fiats, Abarths, and even some Ferraris employed this treatment. The look was most common in the 1950s and early 1960s, but the GTS Coupe is the first modern automobile to update and apply it. *Chrysler*

The GTS Coupe engine may look similar to the original V-10, bit it's virtually a new powerplant. Improvements include lighter castings, revised heads, better cooling, and 450 horsepower. The new engine is about 80 pounds lighter than the original. Insiders say this mill will likely be standard, or at least optional, for the 1997 RT/10 roadster. *Bill Delaney*

just above the wheels. The wheel design made it from prototype to production virtually unchanged, and is offered in a polished-only finish. A particularly neat touch is the Viper-logo-shaped, center-mounted stop light. All glass is tinted, and the rear window opens hatch-style.

Did we say glass? There's more of it now too: A closed coupe body means side windows, power actuated no less! But now there are door handles; lock/unlock is handled electronically via the key fob. The GTS cockpit received Viper's first interior remodeling. The dash is of a different instrument and control layout, and features dual airbags. Credit Chrysler's inte-

rior designers for an exceptionally handsome integration of these safety devices . . . the steering wheel still retains a proper sporty look. Revised leather seats include a pump-up lumbar-support feature, and a more powerful stereo system includes a CD player. It's clear that luxury is a more important element of the GTS's mix than it is in the roadster.

GTS also meant big news underhood: a virtually complete redesign of the Viper V-10, which is about 80 pounds lighter than the original, and is rated at 450 horsepower and 490 pounds-feet of torque. Head and block castings are new, and eliminate the aforementioned

The GTS Coupe's interior features a revised steering-wheel boss incorporating an airbag system; a passenger-side airbag is also an element of the revised dash. *Bill Delaney*

coolant delivery tubes outside the engine. A lighter forged crankshaft rides in cross-bolted main bearings.

The NACA duct in the hood is part of a cold-air intake system, which comprised new manifolding, a redesigned air-filter package, and even a water separator to avoid water getting up the GTS's nose. All of the suspension changes made to the 1996 RT/10 carry over to the GTS. Initially, the only color combination offered was metallic blue with white stripes.

The Viper GTS Coupe will just be on the market as this book rolls off the press, but an early sales success is virtually ensured. It has been in the public eye for some time, and there is assuredly pent-up demand. The GTS will surely add another dimension to the Viper line-up and satisfy those who want the performance and the image but with more luxury . . . and without the wind in the hair.

GTS-R

It's the oldest saw in the business: "Win on Sunday, Sell on Monday." One look at the GTS tells you it was meant to be a race car. As discussed, it's clearly cast in the mold of the Cunninghams and Cobra Daytonas (especially the one-off, 427-powered Type 65) of the past, so Chrysler elected to take the obvious step: make a race

Wind tunnel testing the aerodynamics of the GTS-R. A story in *AutoWeek* magazine discussed some of the GTS-R's early teething problems, but this is to be expected with any new racing program. Further development to the GTS-R's shape and cooling have made the car more stable and reliable at speed. *Chrysler*

version! The GTS-R is a limited production racing Viper that will be offered for sale to private teams. It is designed to compete in international GT-class competition, homologated for ACO, IMSA, and FIA events. According to Bob Lutz, "This is a no-holds-barred competition car for the world's great events such as the 24 Hours of Daytona and the 24 Hours of LeMans. It is . . . perhaps the only [production-derived racing car] devel-

oped, produced, and sold directly from an American manufacturer through its own organization."

Honchoing the development of the GTS-R is Team Viper member (and SCCA national driving champ) Neil Hanneman, and the development partner/supplier Reynard Racing Cars, a highly successful constructor for several racing series such as IndyCar and F3. The GTS-R was introduced to the media in August 1995.

Bob Lutz introduces the GTS-R to the media in August 1995 in Monterey, California. He commented that "it will have the potential to take on vehicles such as the McLaren F-1 GTR, at hundreds of thousands of dollars less." True enough; a Viper GTS-R is projected to cost $200,000 . . . a McLaren GTR comes in at well over $1 million. *Matt Stone*

The basic GTS Coupe's steel spaceframe is retained and strengthened via CAD design enhancements and the integration of a roll-cage structure. Exterior coachwork maintains most of the stock car's dimensions, but the GTS-R body is rendered in carbon fiber. One must wonder how many GTS-R–styled rear wings will end up on street Vipers. The carbon-fiber dash panel carries standard instrumentation, and an otherwise stripped interior also contains an on-board fire-extinguisher system.

For power, special dry-sump versions of the V-10 are constructed in three different states of tune with factory offered ratings of 525, 650, and 700 horsepower; the base version was engineered in-house by Team Viper, the latter two were developed in cooperation with Caldwell Development Inc. A racing version of the production Borg-Warner T-56 six-speed manual helps deliver power through an alloy-cased Dana rear end. A combination of stock and specially built pieces comprise the suspension, and Michelin racing slicks, BBS modular wheels, and Brembo disc brakes round out the rolling stock. All yours for a mere $200,000.

As of this writing, the GTS-R had gotten its first taste of competition in the 1996 Rolex 24 Hours of Daytona. Running in the GT-1 class, the cars demonstrated class-leading speed in practice qualifying 17th and 30th overall. The #97 Sifton/Robinson/Seibert entry was involved in an accident on lap 157 and retired. The Cobb/Dinsmore/Hendricks #98 GTS-R battled with transmission and braking problems throughout the race, but was running at the end and finished 29th overall. Not exactly a win, but an honest showing for an all-new car, and the lessons learned will surely be applied as the GTS-R program continues.

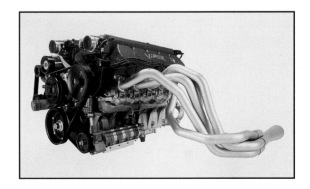

This GTS-R engine rendering shows the dry sump and the long tube exhaust headers; it is based on the new GTS Coupe V-10, and is rated at 525 horsepower in *base* form. *Chrysler*

The Viper GTS-R interior is all business. The dash resembles the shape of the new GTS Coupe unit, but the GTS-R's dash is rendered in carbon fiber. The red handles to the lower right are for the on-board fire-extinguisher system. *Chrysler*

The Future

A further revised RT/10 is set to come forward in 1997. Those in the know say that the 450-horsepower V-10 from the GTS will be standard, or at least optional, on the roadster. The Coupe's revised dash, air bags, and possibly roll-up windows may make the mix as well. More color schemes are in the works.

One thing that's clear is that there will be a Viper for some years to come. It has proven a large U.S. corporation's ability to develop niche products and has validated the concept of the cross-functional team as the way to do it. The Viper has electrified the people who have bought them with nearly frenetic enthusiasm. It has proven a magnificent marketing tool, continuing to garner giggle-infested road tests from the media, and its excitement image has rubbed off well onto other Chrysler products.

For whatever the Viper is or is not, however good it may be or in whatever way it is flawed, it is one of the 1990s' ultimate ways for a driver to embrace the call of the open road . . . a basic element of *freedom* itself.

Indianapolis Motor Speedway President Tony George and Bob Lutz introduce the 1996 Viper GTS Coupe as the official pace car of the 1996 Indianapolis 500. Dodge, perhaps, could not have picked a more interesting and controversial year to pace the race, as it will be remembered as the first race held under the cloud of the CART-IRL dispute. Nineteen ninety-six is the second time a Viper has paced the 500 in five years, this time with Bob Lutz at the wheel. *Matt Stone*

An important group of men in the Viper's history. From left: Bud Liebler, Chrysler vice president of marketing and communications; Marty Levine, Dodge Division general manager; Roy Sjoberg, executive engineer, Team Viper; Tony George, president, Indianapolis Motor Speedway; Neil Hanneman, project manager, Viper GTS-R; and Tom Gale and Francois Castaing, two of the Vipers "Fourfathers." *Matt Stone*

Viper Quarterly

Produced by the J. R. Thompson Company for the Dodge Division of Chrysler Corporation.

VQ is not a book, but a high-quality owner's/enthusiast's magazine published four times a year. It contains a high concentrations of color art, interviews with Team Viper members, light technical information, as well as lots of news, letters, and photos from Viper owners. Well worth subscribing to. Contact: *Viper Quarterly*, P.O. Box 2117, Farmington Hills, MI 48333.

Viper: Pure Performance by Dodge

From the editors of *Consumer Guide*. Published in 1993 by Publications International Ltd., 7373 N. Cicero Ave Lincolnwood, IL 60646.

This is the first book ever published solely on the Viper. It focuses primarily on the early days of the car's development and debut in 1992. There are good archival photos of the prototypes, the first Viper assembly plant, comparisons with other big-inch sports cars, and details on the "team concept" then just spawning at Chrysler. Given the time when this volume was published, it should come as no surprise that virtually every production car shown is red; colors and the GTS were yet to come. Still, this handsome hard-bound volume is easy reading, and worth having.

Dodge Viper On the Road

Compiled by R. M. Clarke. Published by Brooklands Books, Ltd., Surrey, England.

Books usually reflect on specific automobiles or entire marques from a historical perspective, but enthusiast magazines focus on cars as they come out, with an emphasis on road testing. This volume is a collection of reprinted articles and road tests from most well-known buff magazines: *Road & Track, Car and Driver, Motor Trend*, and the like. The pages are all black and white, and being reprints, the graphics are only fair. But the information is solid, and it's fun to compare the road-test performance results. Still in print as of this writing, and a lot of info for the money.

Training Binder

Published by Chrysler Customer Satisfaction and Vehicle Quality Department.

This binder containing seven mini shop manuals is for the serious Viper enthusiast or owner, but the depth of technical and maintenance information is top quality. Available from *Viper Quarterly* or your Dodge dealer.

Viperbilia

Chrysler and Dodge Marketing publishes several catalogs of their own items, as well as collectibles produced by several other firms. Die-casts, promotional models, radio-control cars, clothing, posters, plates—you name it. Contact MIC Corporation, P.O. Box 877, Troy, MI 48099, or call 1-800-647-2701.

Viper Club of America

Enthusiast clubs just make owning special cars easier, and a lot more fun. "Enthusiasm and people" is what the Viper Club of America is all about, according to its first president, Maurice Liang. As of this writing, there are 15 regional VCOA clubs all around the country, with more in the formational stages. They all feature local events, a club newsletter, information exchange, social gatherings, and the like. For information contact: Viper Club Of America, c/o J. R. Thompson Company, P.O. Box 2117, Farmington Hills, MI 48333

Viper RT/10 Production Numbers

1992: 282
1993: 1,403
1994: 3,086
1995: 1,577
Total 1992–1995: 5,988
1996: 710
Source: Chrysler Corporation

Specifications/Data Panels

1992–1995 Dodge Viper RT/10
Dimensions
Overall Length (inches): 175.1
Wheelbase (inches): 96.2
Width (inches): 75.7
Height (inches): 43.9
Track F/R (inches): 59.6/60.6
Curb Weight (pounds): 3,476

Engine
Number of Cylinders: 10
Layout: 90-degree V, OHV
Construction: Alloy block and heads
Bore x Stroke (inches): 4.00 x 3.88
Displacement (cubic inches): 488
Compression Ratio: 9.1:1
Horsepower Rating @ RPM: 400 @ 5600
Torque Rating (pounds-feet) @ RPM: 450 @ 3600
Intake/Carburetion: Computer-controlled direct-port fuel injection

Drivetrain
Standard Transmission: Six-speed manual
Optional Transmission: NA
Standard Differential Ratio: 3.07:1

Chassis/Suspension/Coachwork
Frame Type: Tubular space frame
Body Materials: RTM —fiberglass, polyurethane, polypro-pylene, epoxy/mat composite
Brake Type: Power-assisted four-wheel disks, ventilated
Front Suspension: Independent unequal-length control arms; coil-over shock absorbers
Rear Suspension: Independent unequal-length control arms; coil-over shock absorbers
Steering Type: Power-assisted rack and pinion
Turns (lock to lock): 2.4
Turning Circle (feet): 40.7

Wheels/Tires
Front Wheel Size (inches): 10 x 17; aluminum modular construction
Front Tire Size (metric rating): P275/40 ZR17
Rear Wheel Size (inches): 13 x 17; aluminum modular construction
Tire Size (metric rating): P335/35ZR17

Performance
0–30 MPH (seconds): 1.8
0–60 MPH (seconds): 4.6
0–100 MPH (seconds): 11.7
Standing 1/4-Mile (seconds): 13.2 @ 107 mph
Top Speed (mph): 159
Data Source: *Car and Driver*

1996 Dodge Viper RT/10
Dimensions
Overall Length (inches): 175.1
Wheelbase (inches): 96.2
Width (inches): 75.7
Height (inches): 43.9
Track F/R (inches): 59.6/60.6
Curb Weight (pounds): 3,445

Engine
Number of Cylinders: 10
Layout: 90 degree V, OHV
Construction: Alloy block and heads
Bore x Stroke (inches): 4.00 x 3.88

Displacement (cubic inches): 488
Compression Ratio. 9.1.1
Horsepower Rating @ RPM: 415 @ 5200
Torque Rating (pounds-feet) @ RPM: 488 @ 3600
Intake/Carburetion: Computer-controlled direct-port fuel injection

Drivetrain
Standard Transmission: Six-speed manual
Optional Transmission: NA
Standard Differential Ratio: 3.07:1

Chassis/Suspension/Coachwork
Frame Type: Tubular space frame
Body Materials: RTM fiberglass, polyurethane, polypropylene, epoxy/glass-mat composite
Brake Type: Power-assisted four-wheel disks, ventilated
Front Suspension: Independent; cast aluminum unequal-length control arms; coil-over shock absorbers
Rear Suspension: Independent; cast-aluminum unequal-length control arms; coil-over shock absorbers
Steering Type: Power-assisted rack and pinion
Turns (lock to lock): 2.4
Turning Circle (feet). 40.7

Wheels/Tires
Front Wheel Size (inches): 10 x 17; aluminum modular construction
Front Tire size (metric rating) P275/40 ZR17
Rear Wheel Size (inches): 13 x 17; aluminum modular construction
Rear Tire Size (metric rating): P335/35ZR17

Performance
0–30 MPH (seconds). 1.8
0–60 MPH (seconds): 4.6
0–100 MPH (seconds): 10.5
Standing 1/4-Mile (seconds): 12.9 @ 112.0 mph
Top Speed (mph): 165 (est)
Data Source: *Road & Track* (using 1996 prototype)

1996 Dodge Viper GTS Coupe
Dimensions:
Overall Length (inches): 175.1
Wheelbase (inches): 96.2
Width (inches): 75.7
Height (inches): 43.9
Track F/R (inches): 59.6/60.6
Curb Weight (pounds): 3,425 (estimated)

Engine
Number of Cylinders: 10
Layout: 90 degree V, OHV
Construction: Alloy block and heads
Bore x Stroke (inches): 4.00 x 3.88
Displacement (cubic inches): 488
Compression Ratio. 9.1/1
Horsepower Rating @ RPM: 450 @ 5200
Torque Rating (pounds-feet) @ RPM: 500 @ 3600
Intake/Carburetion: Computer-controlled direct-port fuel injection

Drivetrain
Standard Transmission: Six-speed manual
Optional Transmission: NA
Standard Differential Ratio: 3.07:1

Chassis/Suspension/Coachwork
Frame Type: Tubular space frame
Body Materials: RTM fiberglass, polyurethane, polypropylene, epoxy/glass-mat composite
Brake Type: Power-assisted four-wheel disks, ventilated
Front Suspension: Independent; cast-aluminum unequal-length control arms; coil-over shock absorbers
Rear Suspension: Independent; cast-aluminum unequal-length control arms; coil-over shock absorbers
Steering Type: Power-assisted rack and pinion
Turns (lock to lock): 2.4
Turning Circle (feet): 40.7

Wheels/Tires
Front Wheel Size (inches): 10 x 17; aluminum modular construction
Front Tire Size (metric rating): P275/40 ZR17
Rear Wheel Size (inches): 13 x 17; aluminum modular construction
Tire Size (metric rating): P335/35ZR17
Performance not available

1996 Dodge Viper GTS-R
Dimensions
Overall Length (inches): 176
Wheelbase (inches): 96.2
Width (inches): 75.7
Height (inches): 44.1
Track F/R (inches): 59.6/60.6
Curb Weight (pounds): 2,750 (dry)

Engine
Number of Cylinders: 10
Layout: 90 degree V, OHV

Construction: Alloy block and heads
Bore x Stroke (inches): 4.00 x 3.88
Displacement (cubic inches): 488
Compression Ratio: 9.6:1
Horsepower Rating @ RPM: 525 @ 5200
Torque Rating (pounds-feet) @ RPM: 530 @ 3600
Intake/Carburetion: Computer-controlled direct-port fuel injection

Drivetrain
Standard Transmission: Six-speed manual/close ratio; racing
Optional Transmission: NA
Standard Differential Ratio: As required

Chassis/Suspension/Coachwork
Frame Type: Tubular space frame
Body Materials: Carbon fiber
Brake Type: Brembo four-wheel disks, ventilated
Front Suspension: Independent; cast-aluminum unequal-length control arms; coil-over shock absorbers (Koni)
Rear Suspension: Independent; cast-aluminum unequal-length control arms; coil-over shock absorbers (Koni)
Steering Type: Power-assisted rack and pinion

Wheels/Tires
Front Wheel Size (inches): 11 x 18; BBS aluminum/magnesium; three-piece modular construction
Front Tire Size: 27/65-18 Michelin or Goodyear
Rear Wheel Size (inches): 13 x 17; BBS aluminum/magnesium; three-piece modular construction
Rear Tire Size: 30/70-18
Note: Optional 650 and 700 horsepower engines can be provided, based upon customer order.

INDEX